Animals
that Live in
Social Groups

Bobbie Kalman

Crabtree Publishing Compan

www.crabtreebooks.com

Big Science Ideas

Created by Bobbie Kalman

For our friends Lynn and Dave Roselli,
who have mastered the art of "living in our social group"

Author
Bobbie Kalman

Photo research
Bobbie Kalman

Editors
Kathy Middleton
Crystal Sikkens

Design
Bobbie Kalman
Katherine Berti

Print and production coordinator
Katherine Berti

Photographs
Digital Vision: page 22 (bottom left)
Thinkstock: page 12, 16 (brood pouch with chick, brood pouch with egg)
Wikimedia Commons: Ondřej Žváček: page 21 (bottom); Dave Watts: page 21 (top left)
Other images by Shutterstock

Library and Archives Canada Cataloguing in Publication

Kalman, Bobbie, author
    Animals that live in social groups / Bobbie Kalman.

(Big science ideas)
Includes index.
Issued in print and electronic formats.
ISBN 978-0-7787-2787-3 (bound).--ISBN 978-0-7787-2825-2 (paperback).--
ISBN 978-1-4271-8099-5 (html)

    1. Social behavior in animals--Juvenile literature. 2. Animal
behavior--Juvenile literature. I. Title. II. Series: Kalman, Bobbie. Big
science ideas.

QL775.K34 2016   j591.56   C2015-908714-7
                                         C2015-908715-5

Library of Congress Cataloging-in-Publication Data

Names: Kalman, Bobbie, author.
Title: Animals that live in social groups / Bobbie Kalman.
Description: New York, New York : Crabtree Publishing Company,
    [2016] | Series: Big science ideas | Includes index. |
    Description based on print version record and CIP data provided
    by publisher; resource not viewed.
Identifiers: LCCN 2015045726 (print) | LCCN 2015045151 (ebook) |
    ISBN 9781427180995 (electronic HTML) | ISBN 9780778727873
    (reinforced library binding : alk. paper) | ISBN 9780778728252 (pbk. :
    alk. paper)
Subjects: LCSH: Social behavior in animals--Juvenile literature. | Animal
    behavior--Juvenile literature.
Classification: LCC QL775 (print) | LCC QL775 .K35 2016 (ebook) |
    DDC 591.56--dc23
LC record available at http://lccn.loc.gov/2015045726

Crabtree Publishing Company

www.crabtreebooks.com   1-800-387-7650

Printed in Canada/022016/IH20151223

Published in Canada
Crabtree Publishing
616 Welland Ave.
St. Catharines, Ontario
L2M 5V6

Published in the United States
Crabtree Publishing
PMB 59051
350 Fifth Avenue, 59th Floor
New York, New York 10118

Published in the United Kingdom
Crabtree Publishing
Maritime House
Basin Road North, Hove
BN41 1WR

Published in Australia
Crabtree Publishing
3 Charles Street
Coburg North
VIC 3058

Contents

What are social groups?

Animals must adapt in order to stay alive. One of the most helpful adaptations that animals have made is living in social groups. Animals that live in groups help one another find food, care for their babies, and defend against **predators**.

Big and small

Small groups that include a mother, father, and their young are called **nuclear families**. Other families are made up of one male, several females, and their babies. Bigger family groups may include many females and their young. Big social groups often contain several families.

Social group names

Animal groups are called by different names. Some groups are known by several names. Which of these animal group names do you know?

band baboons
conspiracy lemurs
colony penguins
cotery prairie dogs
herd elephants
mob meerkats
pack wolves
pod dolphins, orcas
pride lions
society chimpanzees, bonobos
troop apes and monkeys

Crows fly in large groups looking for dead things to eat.

Name the groups!

Read the clues in the captions and guess which group is called:

- army
- cackle
- zeal
- murder
- tower

If you cannot guess, find animal group names on the Internet.

Hyenas make high-pitched laughing sounds.

The necks of giraffes look like tall structures.

Zebras run with happy energy!

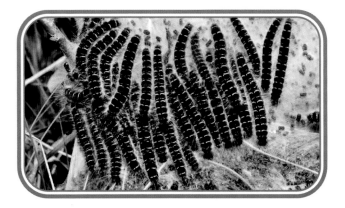

These caterpillars are waging war on plants.

Elephant herds

Elephants live in close family groups called herds. A herd is made up of female adults, called cows, and their calves. Adult males do not stay with the herd. The **matriarch**, or oldest female, rules over the herd, which can have as few as five elephants or more than 50. Elephants eat a lot, so they need to keep moving to find food. The members of a herd eat, sleep, bathe, and travel together. They all help take care of the calves.

The matriarch of the herd shows the young elephants where to find water to drink.

Mothers and calves

Like all mammals, elephant mothers **nurse**, or feed their babies milk from their bodies. As the calves grow bigger, mother elephants teach them which plants are good to eat. The calves need their mothers to survive. All the cows in a herd help take care of the calves.

Sending messages

Elephants say hello by wrapping their trunks together. Touch is an important part of elephant communication.

Elephants communicate by making about 25 calls with different meanings. They also make low rumbling sounds called **infrasound**. People cannot hear infrasound, but elephants can hear it a long distance away.

Elephants make loud calls by blowing air through their trunks. They also stomp their feet to make sounds that can be heard far away by other elephants.

Like people, elephants help one another, even in times of mourning. When a member of an elephant herd dies, the other elephants gather around the body and gently touch it with their trunks and feet. They share their grief and make mournful-sounding noises for days. The elephant above is using its trunk to send messages to other herd members that an elephant has died.

Baby elephants seldom survive when their mothers die.

Your communication

Name some ways you communicate to show:
- you are afraid
- you like others
- you are sad
- you are happy

Wolf packs

Wolves live in social groups called packs, which are made up of parents, grandparents, offspring, siblings, aunts, uncles, and sometimes wolves from other packs. Each pack has a territory with enough fresh water and food for the pack. Its members live together and work as a team to hunt animals to eat. The mother and father are the leaders of the pack. They are called the **alpha** wolves and are the only ones that make babies. After the alphas, wolves second-in-command are called **betas**, followed by **mid-ranking** wolves, and finally the **omegas.**

The wolves on these pages are gray wolves. Other kinds of wolves are red wolves and Ethiopian wolves.

Mother and pups

A mother wolf gives birth to a litter of four to seven pups. She hides the pups in a den for about one month. The pups are safe from predators there. All the wolves in a pack help take care of the pups. When the pups are very small, other pack members bring food to the mother so she does not have to leave the den.

These young pups are in a den with their mother. They leave the den for short periods to look around and play.

A mother wolf is nursing her pups. When the pups are ready to leave the den, they join the pack and learn how to hunt with the other wolves.

Wolf communication

Wolves communicate and share knowledge with one another. Older wolves teach younger wolves how to mark their territories, keep in touch with one another, and hunt with the pack.

Wolves howl to let members of their pack know where they are.

Wolves mark their territories with urine. When wolves from other packs smell these scents, they know that they cannot live or hunt in that area.

*Wolves bare their teeth when they are angry. **Dominant** wolves show the pack that they are in charge by carrying their tails high or holding other wolves beneath them. Weaker wolves show **submission** by lying down or holding their tails between their legs.*

12

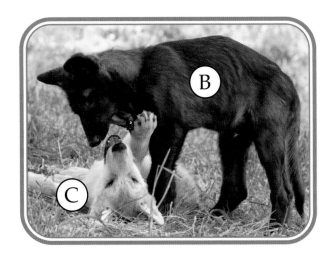

Which one?

Which wolf is: 1. howling 2. angry
3. showing dominance 4. showing submission
5. paying attention 6. showing love

Answers

1.A 2.E 3.B 4.C and G 5.D 6.F

Life in a dolphin pod

Dolphins are very intelligent animals that live in social groups called pods. Living as part of a pod helps dolphins catch food and protect one another from predators such as sharks. Dolphins swim close together and communicate by using movements and sounds such as clicks, whistles, barks, and grunts. Each dolphin has its own special sound, which is like a name. Dolphins recognize one another by their sounds. Not only do they have different sounds, dolphins also have different personalities. They get to know one another by playing. Dolphins love to play!

Dolphins work together to hunt for food. They herd fish tightly together or drive them to shallow water to trap them. They then take turns eating them. Dolphins swim fast and dive deep. While swimming, dolphins surround the calves in the pod to protect them.

Orca pods

Orcas are the largest dolphins. The members of their pods are rarely apart for longer than a few hours. Calves, mothers, and grandmothers often form lifelong family bonds. The older orcas teach the calves how to hunt and survive.

15

Penguin colonies

Penguins are birds that swim but cannot fly. Most penguin species live and breed in huge groups called colonies. Each mother and father pair has a territory, which includes a nest and a small area around the nest. Emperor penguins, shown below, live in cold Antarctica. Instead of building nests, the mothers lay their eggs and then leave to look for food. The fathers keep the eggs warm in **brood pouches**. When the eggs hatch, the fathers also keep the chicks warm in their pouches. After two months, the mothers return with bellies full of food that they **regurgitate**, or bring up, to feed the new chicks. The male emperors then leave to look for food for themselves.

*brood pouch
with chick*

*brood pouch
with egg*

Many penguins live on the frozen ocean in Antarctica, but some live in the oceans around South America, Australia, and Africa. These areas are near the **equator**, where it is hot year round.

Some penguins use loud calls to find their partners or chicks among the thousands of other penguins in the colony. The calls sound like trumpets blaring. Penguins of some species greet one another by bowing, flapping their wings, or waving their beaks in the air.

Chicks touch the beaks of their parents with their own beaks to let them know that they are hungry.

Lion prides

Lions are big wild cats that are part of close-knit social groups called prides. A pride can be small or have as many as 50 members. Together, the lions in a pride find food and protect cubs from predators. One male leads the pride. Lionesses, or female lions, are all related and stay in the pride their whole lives. Younger males often challenge leaders and chase them away. The new leader may then kill the cubs and have new cubs with the females.

*The male lion protects the pride's territory, and the females hunt for food. In a large pride, several hunters can tackle big **prey**. The pride members then share the food.*

Lions live in a grassland habitat called the savannah. Savannahs are in Africa, near the equator, where the weather is hot all year long.

All young male lions must find their own territories and prides once they are old enough to take care of themselves.

This lion cub is learning how to roar. Lions and tigers are the only cats that can roar.

Lion cubs love to play, just as other cats do. They wrestle with one another to practice their hunting skills.

Gelada baboon bands

Gelada baboons are monkeys. Like people, monkeys are primates. Most monkeys live in forests, but gelada baboons live high on mountains in Africa. They sleep on the edges of cliffs at night and look for food on the **plateaus** during the day. Although most baboons eat both plants and meat, gelada baboons eat mainly grass. Their fingers and teeth have adapted to pulling and chewing on grass, flowers, and roots.

Gelada baboons are also known as bleeding–heart baboons. Why do you think that is?

Gelada social groups

Geladas belong to both small and large groups. The smallest is the **reproductive unit**, or family group, which makes babies together. Family groups have up to twelve females, four males, and several young. Bands are made up of two to 27 family units. Larger bands, known as troops, have up to 60 units. The females in family groups have strong bonds and stay in their units for life. Males will stay in a family unit for four to five years and often try to take over other family units. When a new male tries to take over, the females in the group can choose to join him or reject him. There are also all-male groups that spend two to four years together before joining a family.

How many members does the above family unit have? Which do you think is the leader?

Mother geladas feed their babies and carry them on their backs or chests.

*Males **groom**, or clean, the females.*

21

Chimpanzee societies

Chimpanzees use sticks and leaves as tools to catch insects to eat.

Chimpanzees are primates called great apes. Gorillas, orangutans, and bonobos are other great apes. Chimpanzee societies, also called troops, can contain from 30 to 80 chimpanzees, made up of several males, females, and their offspring. Each troop is led by the most powerful male chimp. The troops often fight the chimpanzees in other troops for territory. Sometimes they even eat the infants of the other groups.

Chimpanzees live mainly on the ground, but they sleep in trees.

Bonobos

Bonobos are known as pygmy chimpanzees because they live near groups of people known as pygmys. More intelligent and less aggressive than common chimpanzees, bonobos are the primates that are most like humans. They communicate through calls, but they also use hand signals and facial expressions. They laugh when they are happy and show feelings such as **empathy**. What do you think each of the baby bonobos above is communicating?

Bonobo societies are larger than those of chimps. They contain several males and females, but unlike in chimpanzee troops, the females are dominant.

Gorilla troops

As they mature, males develop a large silver patch on their backs. They are called silverbacks.

When a silverback feels threatened by an attacker, he pounds on his chest, makes loud sounds, and throws plants at his enemy.

Like chimpanzees, gorillas are great apes. There are eastern and western gorillas. Eastern lowland gorillas and mountain gorillas belong to the eastern group. Western lowland gorillas and Cross River gorillas belong to the western group. All gorillas are **endangered**.

Troop members

Gorilla troops are made up of one adult male, or silverback, several females, and their young. The silverback makes decisions for his troop members, leads them to food, and protects them. Younger males, known as blackbacks, help the silverback protect the females and babies of the troop.

A gorilla mother has only three babies in her lifetime, so not many new gorillas are born. The mothers take good care of their babies. They nurse them for up to four years.

Gorillas can catch the same diseases as humans, so people must keep a safe distance from these animals. When gorillas catch human diseases, their bodies cannot fight them, and many die.

Male gorillas have weak social bonds with one another. They leave their groups when they are about eleven years old. They find female partners, make babies, and form new family groups.

Lemur conspiracies

Like monkeys and apes, lemurs are primates. There are many kinds of lemurs, but ring-tailed lemurs are the best-known. They get their name from their long, bushy, striped tails. Ring-tailed lemurs sleep in trees, but they mainly live on the ground. They live in large groups called bands, troops, or conspiracies. The females are the group bosses.

Ring-tailed lemurs like to eat, warm themselves in the sun, and then rest. They often huddle together on the ground to keep warm.

Lemurs have one or two babies at a time. The females in the troop help care for all the babies and will even nurse the babies of other females.

Lemurs hold their tails up while walking so that others in their band can see them from far away.

Only in Madagascar

Lemurs have lived on Earth for more than 62 million years. When the island of Madagascar broke away from the continent of Africa, the lemurs went with it. Lemurs now live only on this island. Many are endangered because their forest homes are being burned down and replaced by farms. Some lemurs are hunted for their meat.

Meerkat mobs

Meerkats belong to the mongoose family and are part of the **Carnivora** group, along with dogs, cats, and bears. They live together in mobs or clans of 20 to 50 members. Meerkats help one another find food, take care of the babies, and guard their homes from danger.

Meerkats are very social and bond with their mobs. They hug, clean one another, and take good care of their young.

Meerkats live in several African deserts in large underground homes with many openings. They take turns as guards, watching for predators. If a guard sees a predator, it lets out a loud alarm call that tells the others to take shelter.

Prairie dog coteries

Prairie dogs are rodents. They live in North American grasslands, on the other side of the world from meerkats, but their lives are very similar. Prairie dogs also live in large underground communities, called towns, which may contain thousands of animals. Their close-knit family groups are called coteries.

Like meerkats, prairie dogs take turns standing guard and watching for predators such as foxes and eagles. Adult prairie dogs teach their young how to find food and stay alive. Prairie dogs also hug and kiss one another.

29

Your social groups

Animal social groups are organized in different ways. Some have male leaders, other groups are made up mainly of females. Social animals communicate using sounds, body language, facial expressions, and hand signals. They teach their offspring in different ways, too.

Family is the most important animal and human social group. Write a story about your family history.

People are social, too

People also have social groups. Our social groups are similar to those of animals. Like animal social groups, our groups also have special names. To which of these social groups do you belong?

- family clans
- school clubs
- dance troops
- religious congregations
- sports teams
- cultural groups
- music bands

How and what are these elephants communicating?

Name six ways that the children below are communicating.

30

Dolphins are very social and love to have fun! Which of your social groups is a lot of fun and makes you feel happy?

Which groups?

Which of your social groups taught or could teach you how to:

- walk, ride a bike, swim
- read, write, use a computer
- play games and sports
- dance, sing, play music
- keep healthy
- learn about your culture
- defend yourself

These children belong to a martial-arts club. They take karate lessons to have fun, feel confident, learn self-defense, and make new friends.

Meerkats take turns guarding their communities. Who keeps your community safe? Which groups keep your country safe?

31

Glossary

Note: Some boldfaced words are defined where they appear in the book.

brood pouch The pouch on the bodies of certain animals, used to protect eggs or young

Carnivora A group of meat-eating mammals

dominant Describing an animal that controls or commands others

empathy The action of understanding and being sensitive to the feelings of others

endangered Describing a plant or animal that is in danger of dying out

equator An imaginary line around the center of the Earth, where the weather is hot year round

groom To clean another animal's fur

infrasound Sound vibrations that cannot be heard by humans

matriarch A female that rules over a social group

nurse To feed a baby milk from a mother's body; to drink milk from a mother's body

plateau An area of high, flat land

predator An animal that hunts and eats other animals

prey An animal that is hunted by a predator

regurgitate To bring food back up; vomit

submission The act of letting another person or animal be in control

Index